A DVD-based Study Series
Study Guide

MARK

Hope for the Gentiles

With Michael Card

A DVD-based study series
Study Guide

MARK

Hope for the Gentiles

With Michael Card

Seven Lessons for Group Exploration

DISCOVERY HOUSE

P U B L I S H E R S®

Feeding the Soul with the Word of God

The Daylight Bible Studies are based on programs produced by
Day of Discovery, **a Bible-teaching TV series of this ministry.**

© 2014 by Discovery House Publishers

Requests for permission to quote from this book should be directed to:
Permissions Department
Discovery House Publishers
P.O. Box 3566
Grand Rapids, MI 49501
Or contact us by e-mail at permissionsdept@dhp.org

Study questions by Andrew Sloan
Interior design by Sherri L. Hoffman
Cover design by Jeremy Culp
Cover image by Jeremy Culp

ISBN: 978-1-62707-061-4

Printed in the United States of America
First Printing 2014

CONTENTS

INTRODUCTION

Hope for Gentiles—and for All

It was a Gentile—a Roman centurion—who was the first person to acknowledge who Jesus was after His death on the cross. Shortly after Jesus cried out, "Father, into your hands I commit my spirit" (Luke 23:46) and died, this soldier declared, "Surely this man was the Son of God" (Mark 15:39)—perhaps in response to passersby who just earlier had mockingly shouted to Jesus, "Come down from the cross, if you are the Son of God!" (Matthew 27:40).

Contrast the Roman centurion's statement of amazement at what he saw in Jesus with the declaration of the Roman government in 9 BC when Augustus was born: "providence . . . has set forth in most perfect order by giving us Augustus, sending him as savior . . . the god Augustus."

In the day in which Mark and the other gospel writers penned their accounts of Jesus' life, they were presenting a stark contrast to the general feeling of the day in the Gentile world—the one ruled by Roman dominance—that their god was Augustus.

Mark and the others were offering a new hope to the world—a new reality that was based on the evidence they were providing in their Gospels: They were telling "the beginning of the gospel about Jesus Christ, the Son of God" (Mark 1:1). The story Mark was telling was the only true hope for a world under Roman domination—the story of a man sent from God who would bring healing and wisdom as He walked the roads of Palestine—and who would bring ultimate joy and hope when He presented himself as a sacrifice for Gentiles and Jews alike on the cross.

Look at the people who found hope as Jesus and His followers traversed the land of Israel: the disciples who battled a storm on the sea of Galilee, a leper who sought to be cleansed, a demoniac who faced certain death if Jesus had not intervened, a girl who had died despite her father's love, a woman who had bled for a dozen years, five thousand people who needed a meal, a blind man who then followed Jesus.

Hope. It entered into life for all of those people because of Jesus. And as the centurion noticed, it came for all at the cross when Jesus, "the Son of God," died to give hope to everyone—Gentile and non-Gentile alike.

Mark's gospel exudes hope as it reminds us of our Savior's love and compassion for all.

—Dave Branon
Editor

SESSION 1

A Whole New World

DAYLIGHT PREVIEW

The Urgent Gospel

Whether it was because of Mark's own passion or perhaps because of Peter's emotional influence on him, the gospel of Mark breaks forth with urgency. From the first sentence—a monumental announcement of the hope that was presented to the Gentiles at Rome where Mark wrote the book—this record of Jesus' life is filled with action. The book begins with Mark's gospel declaration "about Jesus Christ, the Son of God," and it ends with the disciples' departure to preach this story "everywhere." Indeed, the gospel of hope was urgent, and Mark made that abundantly clear.

—————————— COME TOGETHER ——————————

Icebreaker Questions

1. Have you ever visited Rome? If not, how high is it on your wish list of places to see?

2. Michael Card points out that Barnabas was Mark's cousin. Which cousin(s) did you spend a lot of time with when you were growing up?

3. Michael notes that the first church essentially began at Mark's house. Do you have fond memories of meeting in a home with other Christians?

FINDING DAYLIGHT

Experience the Video

Feel free to jot down Video Notes as you watch the presentation by Michael Card. Use the space below for those notes.

─────────────────── **VIDEO NOTES** ───────────────────

Two-part book

Who was Mark?

Rome

Mark's credentials

Peter fled to Mark's house

Church starts there

Barnabas' cousin

Travels with Paul

Close relationship with Peter

Mark: The gospel of Peter

Mamertine Prison

Built as a cistern

Became a prison

Paul and Peter possibly held there

Mark: An emotional gospel

Sixteen adjectives describing the emotional life of Jesus

Jesus holds children

Urgency of this gospel

"Immediately" a common word

Suffering is becoming a reality

WALKING IN THE DAYLIGHT

Discussion Time

---DISCOVER GOD'S WORD---

Discussion/Application Questions

1. What does Michael Card mean when he refers to Mark as a two-part book that's based on confession?

2. Michael points out that the Roman emperor Augustus was described as a "savior" and "god," and his birthday "was the beginning of the good news (or gospel) to the world."

   In light of that, how would Mark 1:1 be received by the Roman world in general and by Christians and the Roman authorities in particular?

3. A number of passages in the New Testament provide at least possible background information regarding Mark (who was also known as John).

   - Mark may have been the young man mentioned on the occasion of Jesus' arrest. Read Mark 14:48–52.
   - The Last Supper may have been celebrated in the upper room of the home of Mark and his mother, Mary. Read Mark 14:12–16.
   - This home may have been the same place where Jesus' followers met after His ascension. Read Acts 1:12–14.
   - The believers met at the home of Mark and his mother to pray for Peter after he was arrested by King Herod. Peter went there after being miraculously delivered from prison. Read Acts 12:11–12.

As Michael says, the church started in Mark's house. How would that contribute to Mark's credentials to write a gospel account?

4. **As the following passages show, Mark didn't remain merely in the shadows of the books of the New Testament.**

- We know from Colossians 4:10 that Mark was the cousin of Barnabas, one of the first leaders of the early church. When Barnabas and Paul (who was still known as Saul at the time) began their first missionary journey, they took Mark, or John, with them. Read Acts 12:25–13:4 and 13:13.
- We don't know why Mark left Paul and Barnabas, but that decision later led to a sharp disagreement between the two men. Read Acts 15:36–40.
- Nevertheless, about fourteen years after Mark deserted Paul and Barnabas, we can see that the relationship between Paul and Mark had been restored. Read Colossians 4:10.
- And about seven years later, during Paul's final imprisonment leading up to his execution, Paul spoke highly of Mark. Read 2 Timothy 4:9–11.

How do you suppose these events and developments shaped Mark as a person and as a gospel writer?

5. **Michael notes that one of the most important aspects of Mark's background and story was the fact that he had a close relationship with Peter. Read about that in 1 Peter 5:12–13.**

Note: "She who is in Babylon" was probably a cryptic reference to the church in Rome.

What does Peter's remark regarding Mark say about their relationship?

6. What is the significance of the fact, as Michael puts it, that "the gospel of Mark is actually the gospel of Peter"?

7. Michael points out that the book of Mark, though shorter than the other gospels, uses more than twice as many adjectives to describe the emotional life of Jesus as do the others. And only in the gospel of Mark do we see Jesus actually holding children in His arms.

    How does this provide evidence of Peter's fingerprints and influence on the gospel of Mark?

—————————— BRINGING IT HOME ——————————

1. In 1 Peter, Peter refers to Mark as "my son." Have you ever had a relationship with a "spiritual father" or "spiritual mother"?

2. On the other hand, have you ever had a relationship with a "spiritual son" or "spiritual daughter"?

3. Are there steps you should take to develop at least one of those kinds of relationships?

 ## DAYLIGHT ON PRAYER

Spending Time with God

1. How can the group pray for you as you begin this study?

2. Do you have any other prayer requests you would like to share with the group?

 ## DAYLIGHT AHEAD

The images that lie ahead in Michael Card's study of Mark are powerful: A prison that strikes Michael as claustrophobic. A conflagration in Rome that destroys the largest wooden structure ever built. Jesus in the wilderness with wild beasts all around. And the Savior walking on water. All of these pictures await in Session 2 as we learn more from Mark's gospel about the persecution that sometimes interrupts the lives of Jesus' worshipers.

Pamphlet for Hard Times

DAYLIGHT PREVIEW

A Litany of Trouble

As Michael Card makes clear in Session 2, life for many Christians in Rome was marked by trouble of the first order. Imagine, Michael demonstrates, being held in the Mamertine Prison—a dank, dark holding tank unfit for human habitation—as were Paul and perhaps Peter. Imagine knowing that your crazed ruler, who had just burned down part of your city, had turned his madness toward Christians as scapegoats for the fire. Imagine being cast into the midst of wild animals at the Roman games—just for the emperor's entertainment. But behind the scenes through it all—there was Jesus, who knew about persecution and mistreatment, and offered hope and compassion. It was a litany of trouble, but Mark is the pamphlet for hope in hard times.

―――――――――― COME TOGETHER ――――――――――

Icebreaker Questions

1. The Mamertine Prison makes Michael Card uncomfortable because he has claustrophobia. How can you relate?

2. Michael visits the Circus Maximus in Rome. What memories do you have of visiting a large sports stadium as a child?

3. Michael compares the two festivals that were held at the Circus Maximus every July to the Super Bowl. How excited do you get about the Super Bowl?

FINDING DAYLIGHT

Experience the Video

Feel free to jot down Video Notes as you watch the presentation by Michael Card. Use the space below for those notes.

─────────────── **VIDEO NOTES** ───────────────

1 Peter 4:12

Language that suggests fiery trials

Circus Maximus

300,000 seats

Two festivals: Apollo, Venus

July 19, 64 A.D.: A fire starts

Nero uses Christians as scapegoats

Gardens of Maecenas

Nero's decisions as emperor

"How beautiful the flames are"

The need to blame someone

The wilderness

Jesus' baptism

Jesus encounters wild beasts

Attended by angels

Jesus walking on the water

 # WALKING IN THE DAYLIGHT

Discussion Time

—————————— DISCOVER GOD'S WORD ——————————

Discussion/Application Questions

1. Michael Card focuses on the consequences that the Great Fire in Rome had upon the early believers, especially those in Rome. Michael sees a hint of that dynamic in 1 Peter. Read 1 Peter 4:7–19.

What do you think of Michael's theory that the fire in Rome happened between verses 11 and 12?

2. Why, according to Michael, did people accuse Nero of intentionally setting the fire in Rome?

3. Why, in turn, do you suppose Nero chose to blame the fire on the Christians?

4. Assuming the story is true, what does it say about Nero that he stood on top of a three-story building overlooking Rome and commented on how beautiful the flames were?

5. If persecution is the immediate context for the gospel of Mark, how would that affect its tone?

6. In the next scene, Michael has gone from Rome to the wilderness in Israel. The first chapter of Mark records an event in Jesus' life that took place in the wilderness. But before that, Jesus was baptized in the Jordan River. Read that account in Mark 1:9–11.

   a. What effect do you think this experience had on Jesus?

   b. What effect do you think this experience had on those who witnessed it?

7. The Spirit that descended on Jesus like a dove then drove Him into the wilderness. Read Mark 1:12–13, Mark's succinct summary of what happened there.

   Mark is the only gospel that tells us that Jesus was with the wild beasts. What connection does Michael see between Jesus' experience and the notion that Mark was written for Christians in Rome who were suffering persecution?

——————— BRINGING IT HOME ———————

1. Michael concludes this session by reading Mark 6:45–51. Have a member of your group read that passage out loud again.

Michael observes that following Jesus for us too is going to be frightening—and wonderful. How has following Jesus been both frightening and wonderful for you?

2. **Michael refers to the gospel of Mark as a pamphlet for hard times. Are you, or someone close to you, in the midst of hard times?**

DAYLIGHT ON PRAYER

Spending Time with God

1. Pray for each other based on what was just shared.

2. What other prayer requests would you like to share with the group?

As you pray, thank God that you aren't going to experience any kind of suffering that Jesus hasn't experienced or any kind of temptation that Jesus hasn't experienced.

> "Therefore, since we have a great high priest who has gone through the heavens, Jesus the Son of God, let us hold firmly to the faith we profess. For we do not have a high priest who is unable to sympathize with our weaknesses, but we have one who has been tempted in every way, just as we are—yet was without sin. Let us then approach the throne of grace with confidence, so that we may receive mercy and find grace to help us in our time of need."
> —Hebrews 4:14-16

DAYLIGHT AHEAD

Michael Card makes a surprising statement about the ministry of Jesus in Session 3. He says that Jesus' ministry was "out of control." You'll hear about the calling of the disciples, especially Peter, and find out why that was an ominous event—not a cozy one. And then you'll examine the events that Michael suggests made the ministry a bit chaotic as it moved into the area of the Sea of Galilee and especially Capernaum. Was it out of control? Find out what that means in Session 3.

A Command to Follow

DAYLIGHT PREVIEW

Out of Control in Capernaum?

As Michael Card moves on to the Sea of Galilee to discuss the beginnings of Jesus' ministry to His disciples, a couple of surprises are in store for us as we listen. First, whatever Sunday-school picture we had of Jesus calling His first disciples is countered with a new image: Engaging the disciples to follow Him was not a cozy, feel-good story, but an ominous one. And it was not a polite request that they do so—it was a command. And then, once the disciples had signed on and Jesus had begun to minister, according to Michael Card, the early stages of the ministry were "out of control." People came in smothering masses to hear Jesus—and when He began doing miracles, Jesus could barely go out in public to serve. People thronged to Jesus for His miracles and His wise words.

COME TOGETHER

Icebreaker Questions

1. Much of this session takes place at the picturesque Sea of Galilee. What is the most beautiful or noteworthy lake you have visited?

2. Michael also recounts a story from Mark in which Jesus was moved with compassion and then touched and healed a man. Who is the most compassionate person you know?

3. As Jesus ministered in Galilee, He was inundated with people. How do you feel about being in a crowd?

FINDING DAYLIGHT

Experience the Video

Feel free to jot down Video Notes as you watch the presentation by Michael Card. Use the space below for those notes.

───────────────── VIDEO NOTES ─────────────────

Sea of Galilee

Jesus' first sermon in Mark

Peter is the first disciple called

"Come, follow Me"

Not a cozy scene

Jeremiah 16:16

Ministry out of control

Jesus is inundated with people

Capernaum: The crush of the people

Jesus avoids the crowds

Jesus and the leper

Jesus heals the man

Jesus drives the man away

WALKING IN THE DAYLIGHT

Discussion Time

DISCOVER GOD'S WORD
Discussion/Application Questions

1. **Michael Card notes that Jesus' very first words in the gospel of Mark were really a simple sermon. Read Mark 1:14–15.**

   What did Jesus mean by saying, "The time has come, the kingdom of God is near" (v. 15)?

2. **What do you think of Michael's observation that the fact that Jesus began to preach before He called any disciples demonstrated that He didn't need them?**

3. **After Jesus began to preach, He called Peter (referred to as Simon here) and his brother Andrew to become the first disciples. Read Mark 1:16–20.**

   a. How does the fact that Mark 1:16 uses a word that only appears one time in the New Testament—the technical term for casting fishing nets—support the notion that Peter was the source of the gospel of Mark?

b. What is the significance of the fact that Jesus' call to "Follow Me" was not an invitation but a command?

4. **Michael points out that the term "fishers of men" comes from Jeremiah 16:16, which is a judgment passage. Getting caught by a hook or a net has life-changing consequences for a fish! This metaphor speaks to God's transforming power that brings both judgment and death as well as hope and new life.**

How does this fit with Michael's observation that the calling of Jesus' first disciples was in reality not a cozy scene but rather an ominous moment?

5. **Michael states that Jesus' ministry, from the very first chapter of Mark, was out of control; that is, Jesus was constantly covered up with people. Read Mark 1:21–39 to see what happened right after Jesus recruited His first disciples.**

Note: In verse 34 we see the first instance in Mark of what has been called the "Messianic secret." Jesus repeatedly commanded His disciples or other people (or here, the demons) to keep quiet about who He was or what He had done. A common view at the time was that the coming Messiah would work miracles and lead the Jews, as their king, to overthrow the Romans. Rather than to encourage those expectations, Jesus wanted to demonstrate what kind of Messiah He actually was.

a. Why did Jesus become an instant celebrity?

b.   If Jesus was God in the flesh, why do you think He felt the need to pray?

6.   **In the last story in Mark 1, Jesus is approached by a man with some kind of skin disease (which has traditionally been translated *leprosy*). As a result, this man was constantly ceremonially "unclean." Read Mark 1:40–45.**

Note: Most Bible translations, in verse 41, state that Jesus was "moved with compassion." However, some ancient manuscripts of the gospel of Mark say that Jesus was "moved with anger" or "indignant." In this case, Jesus experienced anger because of the physical and social toll of the man's disease.

a.   What eventual consequences did this man's healing have for Jesus' life and ministry?

b.   What mixed emotions do you think Jesus may have experienced as a result of needing to impose the "Messianic secret"?

───────────── **BRINGING IT HOME** ─────────────

1.   **Michael ends this session with this reflection:**

"This scene in the first chapter of Mark is not the Jesus of my imagination: the cozy Jesus—Jesus meek and mild—that I grew up with. I don't like Him sternly warning and driving people away. I don't like it when

He says, later in the gospel, 'How much longer do I have to put up with you?' But Mark doesn't want Jesus to be just a figment of my imagination. He wants me to know the Jesus of the Gospels, the Jesus of Peter's life, the Jesus whose emotional life was complicated and beyond anyone's understanding."

How willing are you to know the real Jesus? Do you have any reservations about doing so?

2. **Michael asserts that the crowds wanted Jesus' gifts—they wanted to be fed and to be healed—but they didn't want to hear Jesus' message.**

   If you're really honest, how guilty are you of being attracted to the benefits of following Jesus apart from listening to what He has to say and obeying Him?

DAYLIGHT ON PRAYER

Spending Time with God

1. What prayer requests would you like to share with the group?

2. As part of your prayer time, renew your commitment to respond to Jesus' command to "Follow Me." And renew your commitment to listen to what Jesus has to say and obey Him—rather than merely following Him to receive the benefits.

DAYLIGHT AHEAD

Caution: Miracles Ahead. In Session 4 of Michael Card's study of the book of Mark, Michael takes us back to Galilee to tell of three amazing miracles that Jesus performed. A demoniac is returned to normal, a woman is healed, and a little girl is raised from the dead. And along the way as the disciples follow Jesus and watch Him in action, they learn valuable lessons about faith and trust in Jesus.

At the Feet of Jesus

DAYLIGHT PREVIEW

No Fear; Just Faith

As Jesus crisscrosses the area around the Sea of Galilee in the section of Mark being examined in Session 4, we see Him interacting with three very different people—three people He healed in far different ways. First, He and His disciples are blown by what Michael Card calls a "demonic storm" to Hippos, where Jesus heals, in dramatic fashion, a man possessed. Then he moves to an anonymous place in the region where a woman is healed just by a touch of Jesus' garment. And finally, there is the heartwarming restoration to life of Jairus' young daughter. There is fear in every story, but faith wins in the end.

COME TOGETHER

Icebreaker Questions

1. We learn from Mark 3 that Jesus' family thought He was out of His mind. When you were growing up, what did you do that made your family think you were "crazy" (or drove *them* crazy)?

2. What's the worst storm you've ever experienced?

3. Have you ever been so busy or consumed by something that you didn't take time to eat?

FINDING DAYLIGHT

Experience the Video

Feel free to jot down Video Notes as you watch the presentation by Michael Card. Use the space below for those notes.

──────────────────── VIDEO NOTES ────────────────────

Bookends between Mark 3 and 6: Unable to eat because of crowds

In between the bookends: Jesus disciples His disciples

Demonic storm

Great wind, great calm, great fear

Mark 5: Three people who fall at Jesus' feet

A demoniac in Gentile territory

Legion: Three to six thousand demons

The man's deliverance and its aftermath

A synagogue ruler in Jewish territory

A bleeding (and therefore "unclean") woman

Jesus raises Jairus' daughter from the dead

WALKING IN THE DAYLIGHT

Discussion Time

DISCOVER GOD'S WORD

Discussion/Application Questions

1. At the beginning of this session, Michael Card mentions two book-ends, in Mark 3 and Mark 6, centered on the fact that so many people were coming and going that Jesus and His disciples didn't even have a chance to eat. Michael notes that between the bookends Jesus was "discipling His disciples." Then Michael focuses on a furious storm that Jesus and the disciples encountered on the Sea of Galilee. Read Mark's account of that storm in Mark 4:35–41.

   a. Why does Michael think this was a demonic storm?

   b. At the end of the story, what were the disciples afraid of?

2. After the storm, Jesus and His disciples sailed to the east side of the lake, to an area populated mostly by Gentiles. Read what happened next, in Mark 5:1–13.

   a. Why do you think the man fell on his knees before Jesus?

b. What could have caused Jesus to feel threatened by the demonic opposition?

3. **Now read the rest of the story, in Mark 5:14–20.**

    a. Why do you suppose the people pleaded with Jesus to leave their region?

    b. Although Jesus didn't let the man who had been demon-possessed go with Him, why do you think Jesus deviated from His previous pattern and encouraged the man to go home and tell everyone what the Lord had done for him?

    Note: The Decapolis ("Ten Cities"), mentioned in verse 20, was a league of cities that enjoyed a measure of autonomy and self-rule. With the exception of Scythopolis (Beth Shan), all of these centers of Greek and Roman culture were east of the Sea of Galilee and the Jordan River.

4. **Jesus and the disciples then crossed back over to the west side of the lake, possibly to Capernaum. Read Mark 5:21–34.**

    a. Why do you think it was important to Jesus to find the person who had touched His clothes?

b. Why do you think the woman was afraid? How did Jesus respond to her fear?

5. **At this point Mark returns to the story of Jairus and his daughter. Read Mark 5:35–43.**

    a. When the people from the house of Jairus say, "Don't bother Jesus anymore, because your daughter is dead," what does that imply about their views of Jesus' power?

    b. Ignoring their skepticism, how did Jesus redefine death?

    c. Why do you suppose Jesus returned to His typical pattern, in verse 43, of commanding people to keep silent about this miracle?

——————— BRINGING IT HOME ———————

1. **Michael summarizes the storm in Mark 4 as "a great wind, a great calm, a great fear."**

    In what way is "the fear of the Lord" a good thing?

2. When has God delivered you from a severe "storm"?

3. Are you going through a storm in some sense now?

 DAYLIGHT ON PRAYER

Spending Time with God

1. Pray for one another based on what was just shared.

2. Do you have other prayer requests you would like to share with the group?

3. Just as Jesus assured Jairus, "Don't be afraid; just believe," Michael whispers this to himself all the time: "No fear, just faith." Try whispering that to yourself as you pray.

> "Three people come to Jesus. Three people fall at his feet: a demoniac who's out of his mind; a woman who's dying, who's literally bleeding to death; and a desperate father who has no hope. And what do they find? They find clarity. They find hope. They find healing. They find life. All those same things are still waiting for us at the feet of Jesus."
>
> — Michael Card

DAYLIGHT AHEAD

In Session 5, Michael Card visits two amazing biblical sites: Bethsaida and Caesarea Philippi. And as he continues his teaching from the book of Mark, we get a glimpse of some important events: two banquets, two miracles, and two questions that Jesus asked His disciples. And from those events, we gain new and valuable understanding about who Jesus was: Christ, the Son of God.

An Eye-Opening Messiah

DAYLIGHT PREVIEW

Helping the Blind to See

It was not just the blind man outside the town of Bethsaida who needed help with his vision. So, apparently, did the disciples of Jesus. As Michael Card tells the story, Jesus' followers were having a bit of a hard time grasping the truth about Jesus—of seeing what they needed to see. When He healed the blind man, that man didn't see completely at first—like the disciples. But then Jesus completed the healing. And then look what happens next. Jesus takes His men to Caesarea Philippi to ask them how their sight is: Do they see who Jesus really is? And Peter gives the answer that shows that they are finally getting it: "You are the Christ." Peter finally sees what we all need to see.

COME TOGETHER

Icebreaker Questions

1. During the video, Michael Card mentions that he is rather speechless, which doesn't often happen to him. How often does that happen to you?

2. Jesus took His disciples quite a way north of Galilee to ask them a very important question. If you're married, what was your pop-the-question context?

3. Although Peter gave the right answer, Jesus charged the disciples not to tell anyone—but rather to keep it a secret. How capable were you of keeping a secret as a kid? How about now?

 FINDING DAYLIGHT

Experience the Video

Feel free to jot down Video Notes as you watch the presentation by Michael Card. Use the space below for those notes.

──────────────────── **VIDEO NOTES** ────────────────────

Two "banquets" in Mark 6

Herod's luxurious palace

Fish and bread on a hillside

Two healing parables

A deaf man

A blind man at Bethsaida

"I see people, like trees walking around"

The reality of the disciples' experience

Caesarea Philippi

A pagan place

Peter's confession

Peter's curse

A high mountain above Caesarea Philippi

Transfiguration

The disciples' fear

Believing before seeing

 WALKING IN THE DAYLIGHT

Discussion Time

─────────────── DISCOVER GOD'S WORD ───────────────

Discussion/Application Questions

1. **This session begins with the second of two "banquets" in Mark 6, the feeding of the five thousand. Read that story in Mark 6:30–44.**

   What does Michael Card mean when he says that the feeding of the five thousand was "one of those 'unmiraculous' miracles of Jesus"?

2. **Michael identifies the next passage he recounts as the first of two bookend healing parables. Read Mark 7:31–37.**

   How would this story flesh out the reality of the disciples' experience?

3. **Now read Mark 8:22–26, the other bookend healing parable.**

   Note: This is the only instance in the Gospels in which Jesus placed His hands on someone twice before that person was healed.

   How might this be a parable, of sorts, regarding the reality of the disciples' experience?

4. **Jesus then takes His disciples quite a way north of Galilee to Caesarea Philippi. Read about that in Mark 8:27–30.**

   a. According to Michael, why would this pagan place make perfect sense for Mark's Roman readers as the setting for Peter's confession that Jesus is the Messiah?

   b. What does Michael mean when he says that Peter was speaking more than he knew?

5. Read what happened next, in Mark 8:31–33.

    a.   How did Jesus begin to "undeceive" the disciples by explaining to them what it really meant to be the Messiah?

    b.   Why do you think Jesus reacted so strongly to Peter's resistance to His words?

6. The next scene that Michael recounts took place on a mountain above Caesarea Philippi. Read Mark 9:2–8.

Added to the confession of Peter that Jesus is the Messiah, Michael observes that God's voice says, "This is My Son. Listen to Him." And then Michael states, "It's so important to understand that first comes the confession and then the proof. A little later on we'll be standing before the cross in Mark, and the priests will look up at Jesus on the cross and say, 'Come down from the cross so that we may see and believe.' They don't understand that it has to be the other way around—that belief has to come before seeing."

Why do you suppose God requires believing before seeing?

───── BRINGING IT HOME ─────

1. **After the scene in which Peter declared that Jesus was the Messiah, Jesus made some weighty statements. Read Mark 8:34–38.**

   Like Mark's readers in Rome, we're called to confess Christ in a culture that is in many ways pagan. How can Jesus' heavy words here encourage us?

2. **The healing of the deaf man and the blind man illustrate the disciples' gradual ability to hear, see, and comprehend spiritual truth.**

   a. Has your recognition of who Jesus is come gradually or in more of a dramatic instant?

   b. What can you do to improve your spiritual hearing and sight?

DAYLIGHT ON PRAYER

Spending Time with God

1. What concerns for yourself, others, or world events would you like the group to pray about?

2. Thank God for the miraculous healing of your spiritual ears and eyes to know His truth and salvation. Ask God to give each member of your group keen spiritual understanding and boldness to make the good confession that Jesus is Lord.

DAYLIGHT AHEAD

You're going to need your traveling shoes for Session 6. In it, Michael begins at Capernaum to talk about the compassion of Jesus for children. Then he journeys away from the Sea of Galilee area to one of the oldest cities in the world—Jericho, where Jesus healed a man who became one of His followers. And finally, Michael goes to Jerusalem, Jesus' ultimate earthly destination. In Jesus' story, Passion Week is about to begin, yet even as He enters the city, He teaches a lesson using a fig tree.

SESSION 6

Capernaum, Jericho, and Jerusalem

DAYLIGHT PREVIEW

A Child, a Blind Man, and a Fig Tree

Oh, the lessons Jesus teaches along the way! As Jesus makes His final journey to the Holy City, the scene of His great sacrifice on our behalf, He continues to teach by both word and action. In Capernaum, He interacts with a child in a way that shows us His compassion. In Jericho, He intervenes for a blind man who turns into a disciple. And in Jerusalem, He indicts a fig tree, which gives us a picture of what He will later see in the temple. Jesus is on the road in Session 6, but He never stops teaching.

COME TOGETHER

Icebreaker Questions

1. How do you feel about holding babies?

2. How much did you argue with your siblings or friends when you were a kid? What did you usually argue about?

3. How "green" is your "thumb"? Are you better at growing plants or killing them?

SESSION 6—Capernaum, Jericho, and Jerusalem   **49**

FINDING DAYLIGHT

Experience the Video

Feel free to jot down Video Notes as you watch the presentation by Michael Card. Use the space below for those notes.

───────────────────── VIDEO NOTES ─────────────────────

Capernaum

    Peter's house

    "What were you arguing about?"

    Jesus takes a child in His arms

Jericho

    Last stop on the way to Jerusalem

Bartimaeus asks for mercy, then sight

Bartimaeus follows Jesus

Jerusalem

Jesus enters Jerusalem

Next day: Jesus curses a fig tree and clears the temple

Next day: The fig tree has withered

The lesson of the leaves

WALKING IN THE DAYLIGHT

Discussion Time

———————————— DISCOVER GOD'S WORD ————————————

Discussion/Application Questions

1. This session begins in Capernaum, where Mark records the first instance of Jesus taking a child into His arms (Mark 9:33–37). Jesus then left Capernaum and began His final journey south to Jerusalem, which included ministry on both sides of the Jordan. After entering the territory of Perea on the east side of the river, Jesus took children into His arms for the second time. Read about that in Mark 10:13–16.

    a. Often ignored, children in the ancient world had no power or status and few rights. What do Jesus' actions here tell us about Him?

    b. What do Jesus' words here tell us about the gospel?

2. **Read Mark 10:17–22 to see what happened next.**

    What does Michael Card mean when he says that this man, commonly referred to as the "rich young ruler," would seem to be a great prospect for a disciple?

3. As Jesus eventually approached Jerusalem, He came to the ancient city of Jericho, about five miles west of the Jordan and fifteen miles northeast of Jerusalem. Read, in Mark 10:46–52, about an incident that occurred as Jesus passed through Jericho.

   a. Why does Michael see Bartimaeus, in contrast to the rich young ruler, as the perfect prospect for a disciple?

   b. What does Michael mean when he says that a prerequisite of becoming a disciple is asking for mercy?

   c. What stands out about the process and result of Bartimaeus' healing?

4. Read Mark 11:1–11, the account of Jesus coming, at last, to Jerusalem.

   In fulfillment of Zechariah 9:9, which prophesied the coming of the Messiah on a donkey colt, Jesus clearly presented himself to Jerusalem, the holy city of Israel, as the Messiah. Luke's gospel tells us that some Pharisees in the crowd told Jesus to rebuke His disciples for their loud celebration, and Jesus responded, "If they keep quiet, the stones will cry out" (Luke 19:40).

   Why do you think Jesus felt that the time had finally come for the Jewish people to embrace Him as their Messiah?

5. **Read Mark 11:12–25 regarding the dramatic events of the next two days.**

   a. Michael points out that the two scenes from the fig tree story serve as bookends for Jesus clearing the temple courts. How does that support Michael's observation that the cursing of the fig tree represents a parable of judgment on the fruitless temple?

   b. What application in regard to the cursing of the fig tree does Jesus himself make in verses 22–25?

——————— BRINGING IT HOME ———————

1. In what way can you relate to the rich young ruler?

2. In what way can you relate to blind Bartimaeus?

3. How can you be more like Bartimaeus and less like the rich young ruler?

DAYLIGHT ON PRAYER

Spending Time with God

1. What prayer requests would you like to share with the group?

2. Spend some time in silent reflection and prayer. Read Mark 11:22–25 silently, examining your heart, your faith, and your relationships. Respond like Bartimaeus did when Jesus asked him, "What do you want Me to do for you?" Say to Jesus: "I want to see."

DAYLIGHT AHEAD

As do all of the gospels, Mark's book ends by telling the story of Jesus' death on the cross. As Michael Card retells this most vital story, he begins at Bethany where Mary anoints Jesus for His death with expensive perfume. From there, Card takes us to Jerusalem and reminds us of key events in Jesus' death: the cross-carrying by Simon, the darkness descending, and the friends of Jesus visiting the tomb. Each of these true stories points to a valuable lesson that all of us who live by faith have come to realize: Faith means that we sometimes have to believe before we see.

SESSION 7

Believing Before Seeing

DAYLIGHT PREVIEW

An Abrupt Ending

Sometimes a theatrical production will end before you are fully satisfied with the outcome. Not all of the loose ends are tied up in a neat bow, and you feel a bit frustrated. According to Michael Card, the book of Mark ends in that way—abruptly. That is a reminder of the value of believing before seeing—of accepting by faith what has been taught without demanding fail-safe proof. Mary anointed Jesus before truly understanding that His death was imminent. Jesus' followers went to His gravesite without knowing or understanding that Jesus was going to rise again. These people believed without seeing the final chapter. And Peter said of Jesus, "Though you have not seen him, you love him" (1 Peter 1:8). Someday the ending we all expect will come, and then we will know for sure what at this time we cannot see.

————————— COME TOGETHER —————————

Icebreaker Questions

1. In Mark 14, Mary anointed Jesus with expensive perfume that Michael Card assumes is a family inheritance that was passed down to Mary. What family keepsake do you possess and treasure?

2. How much do you enjoy working in the kitchen?

3. Is there a loved one's gravesite that is important for you to visit?

 FINDING DAYLIGHT

Experience the Video

Feel free to jot down Video Notes as you watch the presentation by Michael Card. Use the space below for those notes.

―――――――――――――――VIDEO NOTES―――――――――

Bethany, the city of Lazarus

A dinner party at the home of Simon the Leper

Mary pours perfume on Jesus' head

Jesus memorializes her action

The Kidron Valley outside Jerusalem

Simon carries Jesus' cross

Crucifixion at Golgotha

Three taunts

Three hours of darkness

Tearing of the temple curtain; declaration of the Roman centurion

A first-century tomb in Jerusalem

The women's concern about the stone

The young man's message

Mark's abrupt and controversial ending

Believing before seeing

WALKING IN THE DAYLIGHT

Discussion Time

DISCOVER GOD'S WORD

Discussion/Application Questions

1. This session begins in Bethany, just east of Jerusalem, as Michael Card recounts a story from Tuesday of Holy Week. Read how that story began, in Mark 14:1–3.

Although Mark doesn't identify this woman, John 12:1–3 informs us that it was Mary, the sister of Lazarus and Martha. And Luke 10:38–42 provides some helpful background for this story. Read that passage.

How does this story in Luke 10 shed light on what motivated Mary in Mark 14:3?

2. Read Mark 14:4–5 to see what happened next.

If you had been Mary, do you think you would have regretted your actions at this point?

3. Now read the end of the story in Mark 14:6–9.

a. How do you think Mary felt about her actions now?

b. What does Michael mean when he says that Mary's story would now become part of Jesus' story?

4. Michael then moves to the story of the crucifixion, beginning with an interesting detail found only in Mark. Read Mark 15:21 and then Romans 16:13.

How does the apostle Paul's mentioning a man by the name of Rufus in the church at Rome support the idea that Mark's gospel was written for that same audience?

5. **Read how Mark proceeds from there, in Mark 15:22–32.**

How does the taunt in verse 32 demonstrate the Jewish religious leaders' failure to comprehend God's principle of believing first and *then* seeing?

6. Read Mark's account of the death of Jesus in Mark 15:33–39.

Jesus' words in verse 34, spoken in Aramaic, show the intensity of His feelings of being abandoned by God the Father while bearing the sins of humanity. Those standing nearby misunderstood Jesus' cry to *Eloi* ("My God") to be an appeal to Elijah. Many Jews believed that the great prophet Elijah would rescue the righteous in times of distress.

When Jesus cried out with His last breath, the curtain of the temple was torn from top to bottom. This curtain separated the Holy Place, which only the priests could enter, from the Most Holy Place, which only the high priest could enter—and then only once a year on the Day of Atonement.

What is the significance of this rending of the curtain?

7. At the same time, the Gentile Roman centurion who was supervising Jesus' crucifixion declared, "Surely this man was the Son of God!"

What does Michael mean when he says that the tearing of the curtain and the declaration of the centurion are linked?

8. **This final session ends with Michael visiting a first-century tomb in Jerusalem, where he recounts Mark 16:1–8. Read that passage.**

Michael points out that the earliest Greek manuscripts of the gospel of Mark don't include Mark 16:9–20 and the early church fathers don't refer to it. Although some scholars think the original ending of Mark's gospel has been lost, Michael has come to believe that Mark intentionally ended his gospel with verse 8.

What do you think of Michael's view that such an abrupt ending is consistent with Mark's demand that we believe *before* we see?

───── BRINGING IT HOME ─────

1. **Michael concludes this study by quoting Peter, the source of the gospel of Mark. In 1 Peter 1:8, Peter wrote this to believers about their relationship with Christ: "Though you have not seen him, you love him; and even though you do not see him now, you believe in him and are filled with an inexpressible and glorious joy."**

In light of this study of Mark, how do those words impact you and apply to you?

2. **What have you appreciated the most about this study and about this group?**

DAYLIGHT ON PRAYER

Spending Time with God

1. How can the group pray for you as you continue to follow Christ?

2. Do you have any other prayer requests?

3. Those who mocked Jesus on the cross said, "He saved others but he can't save himself!" (Mark 15:31). Conclude your prayer time by thanking God for the truth that Jesus saved others precisely by *not* saving himself!

   "You are the Messiah." —Peter, Mark 8:29 (NIV, 2011)
   "Surely this man was the Son of God!" —Roman centurion, Mark 15:39